Shrimp
For Kids

Amazing Animal Books
For Young Readers

By
Rachel Smith

Mendon Cottage Books
JD-Biz Corp Publishing

Read More Amazing Animal Books

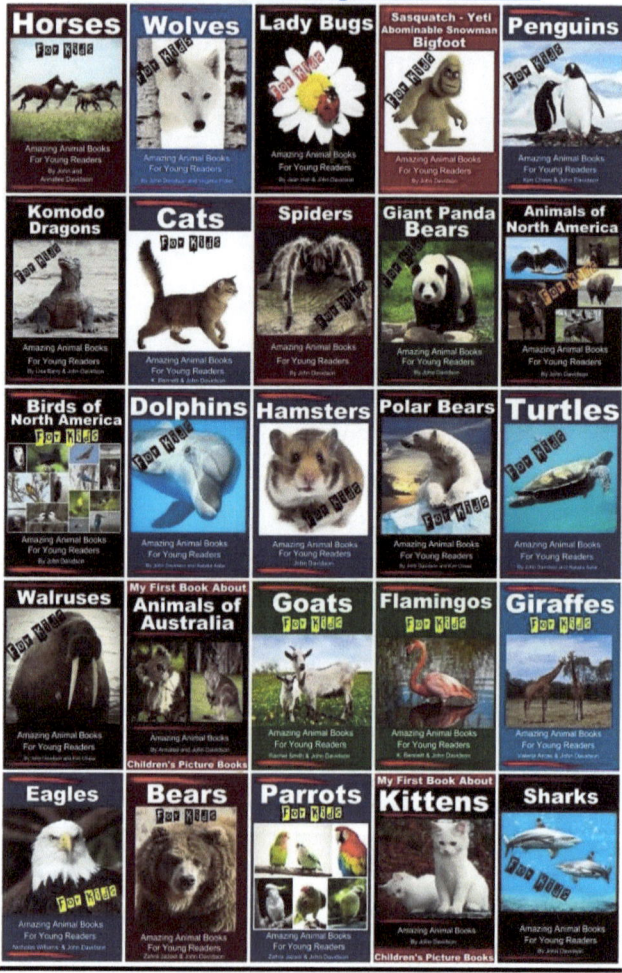

Table of Contents

Introduction

Shrimp are some of the most popular kinds of seafood. You might have seen them at a seafood restaurant, or on TV or in movies. Shrimp seems to be a really luxurious food at some times, and at other times, it's used in things like egg rolls, which are not very expensive most of the time.

However, have you ever wondered what shrimp are like as animals instead of food? There is a whole world of animals within the group name of shrimp. Many kinds of shrimp live throughout the world, and they can be interesting and beautiful to see.

From the itty bitty two centimeter shrimps, to the twenty-five centimeter ones, there is diversity in size and location among the shrimp.

What is a shrimp?

'Shrimp' is not a specific term. It's not scientifically decided exactly what is a shrimp and what is not. But, in a broad term, it means any crustacean (a crustacean is a small water creature with a shell) that has a long sort of body, and that gets around by making a sort of swimming motion.

A red marine shrimp.

The thing with shrimp is that often, for larger shrimp or for other reasons, they can be called prawns. Prawns and shrimp are not scientifically different; they're just different names for the same group of animals.

The word prawn is used for different creatures in different places, so there's no specific difference.

Shrimp have long, muscular bodies. They also have eyes on stalks which can see panoramically, meaning in many directions at once, which is similar to other crustaceans. But one of the big things about them is that they have more developed pleopods than other crustaceans. A pleopod is a special sort of swimming leg, or swimmeret. They also have long slim legs, which are mostly used to perch on things.

Unlike their cousins, the shrimp tends to swim instead of walk. They use their legs and tail to propel themselves along.

A shrimp, at least, of the most common kind, will be divided into two parts: the head and thorax, and the abdomen. The head and thorax, which is basically the chest, are fused together in most shrimp, making up the cephalothorax, which literally means 'head-chest.' This part of the body has a harder shell called a carapace. It's more protected because it's more vital; the chest holds important parts such as the heart.

Also, the carapace protects the gills. Gills are a way of turning the oxygen in the water into something the shrimp can absorb. It's like the water version of lungs in humans or other land-dwelling animals. Some animals have both gills and lungs, or can survive in the air for a while. The shrimp is not usually one of these.

The cephalothorax (remember, the head-chest) has a number of pairs of legs attached. The first three pairs are used for moving food to the mouth. The mouth has a sort of pointed thing above it, and this is where the water is forced into the gills so that its oxygen can be taken.

Then, there's the other legs, which are used for perching.

Meanwhile, there's the long, narrow abdomen. This has a number of legs at each segment; there are six segments, and one pair of legs to each. If you haven't guessed by now, the shrimp has a lot of legs! There legs are used more for swimming. Lastly, there is one little pair of leg-like things called uropods. These allow the shrimp to steer, including being able to go backwards.

Some shrimp use their back legs for brooding, which means taking care of eggs.

One thing that the fanned tail of the shrimp can do is called lobstering. If they are startled, they will lift that tail and bring it down rapidly, sending themselves shooting backwards. This protects them from their predator or whatever else has startled them. It is a very fast reaction.

How do shrimp act?

There are about six hundred kinds of shrimp or so. So, it's nearly impossible to say how all shrimp act. There are big differences between different kinds.

A pair of cleaner shrimp.

Most shrimp are omnivorous, meaning that they'll eat a wide range of things. Some eat parasites from fish, and some eat algae.

Some kinds of shrimp partner up or work with other fish. One kind, the tiger pistol shrimp, often partners up the yellow watchman goby, which is a kind of fish. The two will live together; it'll be the shrimp's job to make and keep the burrow, and it's the goby's job to keep a lookout, because the tiger pistol shrimp is blind.

Pistol shrimps are an example of an unusual shrimp. They have sort of claws, different sizes for each claw. These claws making a loud clicking noise when they use them, and the noise actually often causes problems for underwater recordings. This is because they use the noise to stun prey; often, these noises are called sonic booms. It's one of the loudest noises in the ocean.

Emperor shrimp live on other animals, such as sea slugs and sea cucumbers. These animals allow them to live on them as long as they clear parasites; the parasites are food for the emperor shrimp, and they get protection from being with the sea slug or sea cucumber, so both parties benefit.

Cherry shrimp, which are freshwater shrimp from Taiwan, are very non-aggressive shrimp. They are very popular as pets in Taiwan, and they tend to graze on algae and other materials throughout the day. Interestingly, these are actually not naturally red shrimp; instead, the red shrimp often sold in pet stores are a morph. A morph is a naturally-occurring color in a species, but is not the majority color. An example is the black panther, which can be a black jaguar morph.

Pederson's shrimp, which are pretty, transparent and purple shrimp, live in Bermuda. They are cleaner shrimp, and they tend to live in anemones. This type of shrimp has to immunize itself to the anemone's stings, usually by pressing itself against the parts of the anemone for longer and longer times, until it is used to it.

This shrimp will live in the anemone, though if it leaves for even a few days, it has to immunize itself to the same anemone all over again. Cleaner shrimp, as you might have guessed, clean. They clean fish who stop by their anemone to be cleaned; these fish will stay entirely still for the cleaner shrimp, no fear involved. The cleaner shrimp is getting something out of it too, though: it eats the parasites and such it picks off the fish.

Harlequin shrimp are interesting, because not only are they very colorful, but they only eat one thing: starfish. These shrimp, which live in places like Hawaii, particularly like a big kind of starfish. Harlequin shrimp work in pairs, usually a male and a female, and they don't only mate together, but they hunt together. They flip over starfish, which are very slow, and eat them.

They lay eggs in high numbers, anywhere from 100-5,000 eggs in one season. It really depends on the environment and if the shrimp think their eggs can survive in it.

The pink shrimp, the one you most often see as food at a grocery store, is quite different. For one thing, it starts out as a male, and then becomes a female as it gets older. Because of this, males are almost always smaller than females. Shrimp are very different from humans. They are also called northern shrimp and deep-sea prawn, because they are so well-known among humans who deal with seafood. They are probably the one kind a typical Western human is most familiar with.

Interestingly, shrimp don't just end up eating parasites; they also end up hosting them. Some kinds of parasites, called bopyrid parasites, live in some shrimp. Then, in turn, shrimp are eaten by many creatures, humans included.

Where do shrimp live?

Shrimp live everywhere! Well, everywhere may be an overstatement, but they do live throughout the world.

A harlequin shrimp.

For example, there are several kinds of habitats a shrimp, or rather, a bunch of shrimp, may live in. Coasts are some of the most popular spots; a coast is pretty much anywhere a sea, ocean, or what have you encounters land. This is a pretty fertile place for life, where many fish, crabs, tiny critters, and you guessed it, shrimp, live.

Estuaries, however, are an even better place. What is an estuary, you might ask? It's basically where the freshwater rivers and the saltwater seas meet. An estuary is where some water, usually from the sea but also connected to streams and rivers, is almost surrounded by land.

An estuary has all the tides and other effects of the sea, but also all the sediment and freshwater flow that streams and rivers bring. This makes it a wonderful place for small life to grow, because the water is incredibly full of nutrients. Lots of shrimp and other animals live in these kind of settings.

But shrimp live in other settings too. In the sea, though most live on coasts and in estuaries, some live in the deep sea. The deep sea is where the water gets darker and colder. Humans don't typically go here, as it is incredibly deep down and humans need both oxygen and a different pressure level. Because all that weight of the water, from the top of the ocean down, makes the pressure as you go down stronger and stronger. So, the creatures at the deepest parts of the sea probably could not survive at the top, where we stay, and we could not survive at their pressure.

Another place shrimp live, about a quarter of them, are freshwater places. Freshwater means places like lakes and rivers, without so much salt in the water.

Freshwater and saltwater creatures usually can't switch between the two kinds of water. It's kind of complicated, but because of the salt difference, if one went to the other, it would either get swelled up with too much water, or get all the water pulled out of it. Some, however, can switch because their bodies are adapted to do so. An example of this is the salmon.

What kinds of shrimp are there?

There are a lot of shrimp in the world, more kinds than we could go over in this book even if it was hundreds of pages long. There are, however, several categories of shrimp.

A red crystal freshwater shrimp.

First, there's the two main categories: decapods and non-decapods. Decapods include the more traditional shrimp, mostly the ones that everyone can agree are shrimp.

This includes Dendrobrachiata, which is where many of the shrimp we eat come from. They are also usually larger than other shrimp, which is why we eat them. Sometimes, shrimp from this family are all called prawns to distinguish them from other shrimp.

Then, there's the other group, which mainly includes Caridea and Stenopodidea. Caridea is where the 'true shrimp' belong. Every member of this family is a considered a shrimp without a doubt.

They are also typically pretty small, and we don't eat most of them.

Stenopodidea, however, is where most cleaner shrimp come from. Cleaner shrimp survive by cleaning other fish, eating their parasites and necrotic flesh (which means flesh that's died. It's like when you get a paper cut, and there's that extra bit of skin sticking off).

Then, there are the non-decapods. These are a large group of shrimp, including fairy shrimp, brine shrimp, clam shrimp, and so on.

These kinds of shrimp tend to look a little less like traditional shrimp. For example, clam shrimp look a little like clams, having carapaces (kind of an armor, if you remember) that bend and close.

Then there's the fairy shrimp, which has no carapace, making it vulnerable. It swims on its back, and it is very tiny, so it tends to eat only algae among plankton. Plankton are incredibly small, so you can believe the fairy shrimp is tiny, only a few millimeters, or less than an inch.

Its eggs are actually very durable, surviving during droughts and other disasters to simply hatch when conditions are good. They live in hypersaline lakes, even living in Antarctica, beneath the ice. Typically, they are used to be made into fish food among businesses.

Then there are the seed shrimps. There are about thirteen thousand kinds of seed shrimp, and all are incredibly tiny. They are so named because they look like seeds. A seed shrimp is made up of a clam-like shell that opens and close. Inside is the shrimp, and it opens to feed.

So, as you can see, non-decapods are the more unusual bunch, and so sometimes scientists argue they aren't true shrimp, and that they don't belong in the category. However, for every scientist that says they don't, there's bound to be one that says they do, so the argument will probably go on for a very long time indeed.

The history of shrimp and humans

Shrimp has been a human food for a very long time.

A human family enjoying shrimp.

It sccms Romans enjoyed shrimp, and there have been shrimp-decorated dishes found in Pompeii, a site of ruins that were buried by the volcano Vesuvius a very long time ago.

Evidence suggests that Native Americans of many different areas have been harvesting shrimp for hundreds, if not thousands, of years. They used kinds of nets to scoop them out of the water; there was an abundance of shrimp, so it wasn't hard to catch them.

When the white settlers came to these areas, they didn't know about the shrimp, so while surrounded by food, they starved. It really helps to know your environment, and if they had been friendlier with the native peoples, it's likely they might have learned of the shrimp much sooner.

In the 1700s, the Cajuns, who are the people from France who settled in Louisiana, began to fish the white shrimp that live in that area. They would dry them on the beach, and so it goes on to this day. Shrimp is a big part of Cajun food.

Then, in the 19th century, during the Gold Rush in California, Chinese immigrants were the ones who really kicked off the shrimping industry. Because many of them came from a place, the Pearl River Delta, that had a lot of shrimp, and they were experienced shrimpers, they began to catch the shrimp, which were mostly pretty small, and sell the prepared food to either the Chinese community in California, or all the way back to China.

Unfortunately, the pollution of the gold mining and overfishing put an end to this operation for the most part. Instead, the major shrimping industry moved to the South Atlantic and the Gulf, at least for the United States of America.

Of course, shrimping went on in much of the world, from Asia to the Americas. But it's quite a big industry in America.

Catching shrimp became a big process. This was because both the motor boat and the trawl were combined to capture enormous amounts of shrimp in the 1920's.

This meant that a fast boat could drag a huge net along the bottom of the ocean to catch shrimp in huge numbers. But the problem is, it catches everything else too, and these animals typically just die and get thrown away.

An alternative, which is especially practiced in China, is to farm shrimp. This started mostly in the 1970's, because so many animals were becoming endangered because of trawling.

Trawling still goes on, but now there are more shrimp harvested from farms than come from the wild.

Shrimp as food

Shrimp have long been popular as food. Shrimp and prawn are a world-wide food, eaten in many, many places. It's a staple of seafood.

A shrimp appetizer.

The British, those living in the United Kingdom, tend to call shrimp prawns. Americans tend to call most of the shrimp, shrimp, and very few prawns.

Shrimp is common as a food allergy. It can cause anything from mild irritation to anaphylactic shock, which can be very serious. However, this is not such a common danger that shrimp should never be eaten;

like with peanuts, there just should be a little caution taken for the first time one eats it.

There are religions that ban shrimp. One is Judaism, which bans a number of foods. Interestingly, these rules were made a very long time ago, but most of them reflect the relative danger of such foods. Much of the foods banned by Judaism were more likely to make people sick at the time, due to germs, which of course, the Jews didn't know about. Many modern-day Jews follow this rule.

Some parts of Islam ban shrimp, among other foods. Because there are several kinds of Islam, the rules vary from one kind to the other. However, Sunni and Shi'ite Muslims are banned from eating shrimp.

Shrimp is full of omega-3s, which are good fats. It also has a lot of protein and calcium, both of which are very good for you. Interestingly, it has a high cholesterol level, but unlike other high-cholesterol foods, it actually helps cholesterol problems and circulatory systems. The circulatory system is your heart, lungs, and blood vessels.

Most of the time, shrimp is frozen and sold.

A few interesting and well known dishes include:

Dancing shrimp. This is a dish in which baby shrimp are served alive, usually dunked in sake. This a popular dish in Japan and Thailand, but a lot of people have qualms about eating them alive, understandably.

Dynamite roll. This is sushi, but it's actually Western-style sushi. It has shrimp tempura, which is a kind of fried shrimp, a kind of Japanese fish, and vegetables. It's very popular in Western Canada.

Seafood gumbo. This is a stew or soup that has a bunch of seafood, including crab and shrimp plus a strong stock, vegetables, and a thickener, such as flour and such called roux, in it. It's a very savory dish, and is from Louisiana in America.

Potted shrimp. This is an English dish made from small shrimp and mace-flavored butter. Basically, it's cooked in the small dish, and eaten with bread. The butter helps to preserve it, and often nutmeg and cayenne pepper can be added.

Shrimp roe noodles. This is a kind of noodle made in China. Instead of just the typical noodle ingredients, such as flour, this noodle includes shrimp eggs.

Shrimp as pets and in aquariums

Shrimp are sometimes kept as pets or part of aquariums.

A red shrimp in an aquarium.

Shrimp can be quite pretty in aquariums. They have been bred to come in many colors, from red to blue to yellow, and so if what you're looking for is a very eye-catching tank, then the shrimp can be a great addition.

However, sometimes some kinds of shrimp also come in handy. They may be cleaner shrimp, and help the fish live longer. Others may eat algae, which helps to keep the tank clean.

Shrimp are not as popular in America as tank animals as they are in other parts of the world. For example, in Taiwan, having a shrimp for a pet is not unusual.

Some of the most popular kinds of shrimp as pets are the harlequin shrimp, the cleaner shrimp, the cherry shrimp, the bamboo shrimp, and the Japanese marsh shrimp.

Either saltwater or freshwater shrimp are kept, though generally, among children or less wealthy or dedicated aquarium owners, it tends towards freshwater shrimp.

Conclusion

The shrimp is a fascinating creature, tiny but having such an effect on our world. As food, not just for humans, but also for other creatures in their habitats, they help keep the ecosystem strong. Also, in their roles as predators and as cleaners, they help to balance it as well.

Author Bio

Rachel Smith is a young author who enjoys animals. Once, she had a rabbit which was very nervous, and chewed through her leash and tried to escape. She's also had several pet mice, which were the funniest little animals to watch. She lives in Ohio with her family and writes in her spare time.

Publisher

JD-Biz Corp

P O Box 374

Mendon, Utah 84325

http://www.jd-biz.com/

Mendon Cottage Books
P O Box 374, Mendon Utah 84325

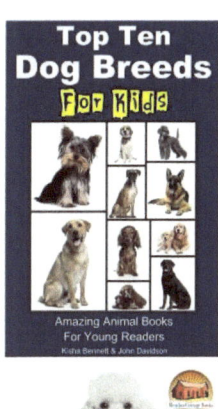

Top Ten Dog Breeds For Kids

Amazing Animal Books For Young Readers

German Shepherds

Dog Books for Kids
K. Bennett

Bulldogs

Dog Books for Kids
K. Bennett

Dachshund

Dog Books for Kids
K. Bennett

Poodles

Dog Books for Kids
K. Bennett

Labrador Retrievers

Dog Books for Kids
K. Bennett

Rottweilers

Dog Books for Kids
K. Bennett

Boxers

Dog Books for Kids
K. Bennett

Golden Retrievers

Dog Books for Kids
K. Bennett

Puppies

Dog Books For Kids

Amazing Animal Books
By John Davidson

Beagles

Dog Books for Kids
K. Bennett

Yorkshire Terriers

Dog Books for Kids
K. Bennett

Dogs
Top Ten Dog Breeds For Kids

Amazing Animal Books For Young Readers
Zahra Jazeel & John Davidson

Cats For Kids

Amazing Animal Books For Young Readers
K. Bennett & John Davidson

Foxes For Kids

Amazing Animal Books For Young Readers
Zahra Jazeel & John Davidson

Wolves For Kids

Amazing Animal Books For Young Readers
By John Davidson and Virginia Fidler

www.ingramcontent.com/pod-product-compliance
Lightning Source LLC
Chambersburg PA
CBHW050912290526
45792CB00002B/794